The Gift of
Assurance

Michael Seed

FOREWORD BY
HRH The Duchess of Kent

continuum
LONDON • NEW YORK

Dedicated to the life and memory of
Cardinal Basil Hume, O.S.B, O.M.
(1923-1999)

Continuum
The Tower Building
11 York Road, London SE1 7NX
370 Lexington Avenue, New York, NY 10017-6503

This edition published by Continuum 2003

© 2000 Continuum International Publishing

**This book contains extracts from *Assurance - An Anthology*,
Edited by Michael Seed, Continuum, 2000.**

British Library Cataloguing-in-Publication Data
A catalogue record for this book is available from the British Library.

Edited designed and produced by
Delian Bower and Vic Giolitto

ISBN 0 8264 6851 9

Printed in Hong Kong

THE DUCHESS OF KENT

In this turbulent world we are all in need of re-assurance. In the pages of this book you will find words which have encouraged, comforted and inspired many.

It is hoped that these same words will bring great peace of mind to the readers - both in everyday life and in times of anxiety.

PREFACE

I remember being taken by my mother to school for the first time, forty years ago and being left feeling anxious and abandoned in the playground. I comforted myself with the thought that, God willing, I would make it home safely where, after a hug, jelly and ice cream, all would be well. I soon realised that I would go back the next day and might just be able to cope. Little did I know that jelly would one day become gin!

From the vantage of adulthood, the problems of five-year-olds can seem slight and transient. In comparison, our grown-up troubles can seem permanent, intractable and, at times, create a deep need for comfort and encouragement. This book is a collection of texts that have inspired people seeking assurance.

I am indebted to the contributors to this edition and hope that it will provide a source of comfort to those enduring suffering and seeking peace. I am particularly grateful to the Duchess of Kent for her kindness in writing the Foreword to this anthology. The Duchess is a dearly loved lady whose actions and words have given me, and countless others, assurance.

I would like to thank Delian Bower for his enormous work in bringing this edition to publication. I am indebted to Vic Giolitto for designing this book. The royalties from the sale of this edition will assist the work of the Franciscan Friars of the Atonement, a religious Order founded in 1898 to further ecumenical and inter-faith understanding,

May God bless you all

Michael Seed

Christmas Day
2002

PETER ALLISS, *broadcaster*

Dear Father Michael

I offer you the following:

'I would be true for there are those who trust me. I would be pure for there are those who care. I would be strong for there is much to suffer. I would be brave for there is much to dare. I would be friend of all, the foe, the friendless. I would be giving and forget the gift. I would be humble for I know my weakness. I would look up and laugh and love and live.'

I hope these few words are worthy. They have been of comfort to me on several occasions over the past 20 years.

Sincerely

ANONYMOUS

Long ago, in the East, it was common practice for carpet-weavers to sit in the market place working away at their looms. They wove wonderful pictures and patterns into their carpets, but while the work was in progress, only the weaver could see them. Anyone looking at the back of the carpet would have seen only a very untidy-looking hotch-potch of colours, but the weaver knew exactly what he was doing. Someone wrote a verse which likens God to the weaver, working out his design on the canvas of our lives.

It goes like this:

Then shall I know

Not till the loom is silent and the shuttles cease to fly
Shall God unroll the canvas and reaveal the reason why.
The dark threads are as needful in the weaver's skilful hand
As the threads of gold and silver in the patterns he has planned.

Traditional

LADY ASTOR,
former model and widow of Lord Astor of Hever

Dear Father Michael

Thank you for asking me to contribute to *The Gift of Assurance*. The text which immediately springs to mind is from *Le Milieu Divin* by Teilhard de Chardin which goes as follows:

'God, in all that is most living and incarnate in Him, is not far away from us, altogether apart from the world we see, touch, hear, smell, and taste about us. Rather He awaits us every instant in our action, in the work of the moment. There is a sense in which He is at the tip of my pen, my spade, my brush, my needle - of my heart and of my thought. By pressing the stroke, the line, or the stitch, on which I am engaged, to its ultimate natural finish, I shall lay hold of that last end towards which my innermost will tends. Like those formidable physical forces which man contrives to

discipline so as to make them perform operations of prodigious delicacy, so the tremendous power of the divine attraction is focused on our frail desires and microscopic intents without breaking their point. It sur-animates; hence it neither disturbs anything nor stifles anything. It sur-animates; hence it introduces a higher principle of unity into our spiritual life, the specific effect of which is - depending upon the point of view one adopts - either to make man's endeavour holy, or to give the Christian life the full flavour of humanity.'

Yours with love

BERYL BAINBRIDGE. *novelist*

To the Franciscan Friars,

Many years ago I bought a second hand paperback entitled *Mediaeval Latin Lyrics*, translated by Helen Waddell and first published in 1929.

There was one poem in particular, by Venantius Fortunatus, that I found haunting, and still do. Having learnt it by heart so long ago, I often recite it to myself, for, with its reminder of mortality, it fits both good times and bad. I know nothing about Greek literature, nor do I understand Latin, but the names give me comfort, and Waddell gives the Latin text beside the translation, the first line being,
'Tempora lapsa volant, fugitivis fallimur horis…

Time that is fallen is flying, we are fooled by the passing hours…
Likeness is none between us, but we go to the selfsame end.
The foot that has crossed the threshold shall no man withdraw again.
…What help in the arms of the fighters? Hector, and vengeful Achilles

Fallen, Ajax is fallen, whose shield was the wall of
Greece.
Beauty, beauty passeth, Astur the fairest is fallen,
Low Hippolytus lieth, Adonis liveth no more.
And where are the songs of the singers? Silent for all
their sweetness.
Small joy to be won in prolonging the notes of
the song.
Even as the moments are dying, the present is flying,
the dice are snatched from our hands and the game
is done.
Naught but the deeds of the just live on in a flower
that is blessed;
Sweetness comes from the grave where a good man
lieth dead.'

With all good wishes

CONRAD BLACK, *newspaper proprietor*

Dear Father Seed,

In response to your request, I think the words of Cardinal Newman's Prologue to *The Second Spring* are ones which I find inspirational as well as comforting.

'We have familiar experience of the order, the constancy, the perpetual renovation of the material world which surrounds us. Frail and transitory as is every part of it, restless and migratory as are its elements, never ceasing as are its changes, still it abides. It is bound together by a law of permanence, it is set up in unity; and, though it is ever dying, it is ever coming to life again. Dissolution does but give birth to fresh modes of organization, and one death is the parent of a thousand lives. Each hour, as it comes, is but a testimony, how fleeting, yet how secure, how certain is the great whole. It is like an image on the waters, which is ever the same, though the waters ever flow. Change upon change, - yet one change cries out to another, like an alternative Seraphim, in praise and in glory of their Maker. The sun sinks to rise again; the day is swallowed up in gloom of the night, to be born out of it, as fresh as if it had never been quenched. Spring passes into summer, and through summer and autumn into winter, only the more surely, by its own ultimate return, to triumph over that grave, towards which it resolutely hastened from its first hour. We mourn over the blossoms of May, because they are to wither; but we know, withal, that May is one day to have its revenge upon November, by the revolution of that solemn circle which never stops, which teaches us in our height of hope, ever to be sober, and in our depth of desolation, never to despair.'

I hope you judge this suitable and send you every good wish.

Yours.

LADY ELIZABETH BASSET,
Editor, Love is My Meaning *(1973), former Lady in Waiting to Queen Elizabeth the Queen Mother*

Dear Father Michael,

I am so delighted to hear you are compiling an anthology. I think *Love is My Meaning* has met a need in these hectic times when people don't have time to read long books. Its contents come from other men's writings all of which brought me comfort in my darkest days.

I think one of the texts that has meant a great deal to me comes from Gerard Manley Hopkins.

'We all have this one work to do
To let God's Glory through.'

It seems to make all one's rather pathetic efforts so infinitely worth while.

Yours ever

SISTER WENDY BECKETT, *author, broadcaster and art expert*

Dear Father Michael,

You ask for the text which most gives me assurance, but I don't really think there is one. My assurance - which is absolute - comes from Jesus Himself: His living Presence. But this is the text I most think of:

1 Corinthians 1, 30:
Christ Jesus 'has become our wisdom and our virtue and our holiness and our freedom'.

Affectionately

Sister Wendy

TONY BENN, *politician*

Dear Fr Michael,

Just a line to send the quotation below which
I hope will do.

Lao Tzu on Leadership

Go to the people
Live amongst them
Start with what they have
Build on what they know
And when the deed is done
The mission accomplished
Of the best leaders
The people will say
'We have done it ourselves.'

With best wishes,

TONY BLAIR, *British Prime Minister*

Dear Michael,

My most inspiring and encouraging text is from St Mark's Gospel, Chapter IV. It is the passage where Christ calms the storm:

4:36   And when they had sent away the multitude, they took him even as he was in the ship.
And there were also with him other little ships.
4:37   And there arose a great storm of wind, and the waves beat into the ship, so that it was now full.
4:38   And he was in the hinder part of the ship, asleep on a pillow: and they awake him, and say unto him, Master, carest thou not that we perish?
4:39   And he arose, and rebuked the wind, and said unto the sea, Peace, be still. And the wind ceased, and there was a great calm.
4:40   And he said unto them, Why are ye so fearful? how is it that ye have no faith?
4:41   And they feared exceedingly, and said one to another, What manner of man is this, that even the wind and the sea obey him?

Yours ever

Tony

MICHAEL BLAKEMORE, *actor and director*

Dear Father Michael,

Work is not the whole of life, but if you're lucky enough to care about what you do, it can comprise a very important part. My work is mainly in the theatre, an absorbing world but not one renowned for its modesty, patience or lack of hysteria.

The following words of Anton Chekhov, written to his actress wife, are the best advice I've ever read to someone trying to make their way in the Arts (or, come to think of it, in anything else). We should all learn them by heart.

> 'You must stop worrying about success or failure, your business is to work step by step, from day to day, softly-softly, so be prepared for unavoidable mistakes and failures, in a word, follow your own line and leave competition to others.'

With every good wish

Michael Blakemore

RABBI LIONEL BLUE, *author and broadcaster*

22.5.00

Dear Michael

It is with pleasure I send you the following, written by an unknown child in a Nazi death camp. (From *Forms of Prayer, Days of Awe* p. 807 RSGB)

> 'From tomorrow on I shall be sad
> From tomorrow on, not today.
> Today I will be glad and every day
> no matter how bitter it may be
> I shall say
> From tomorrow on I shall be sad
> Not today.'

God bless

Yours

CHERIE BOOTH, *barrister*

Dear Father Michael

You asked me to send you a text which has inspired or encouraged me or given me strength in times of difficulty.

I have always found the Magnificat a beautiful part of St Luke's Gospel. It is the words Mary spoke when visiting her kinswoman Elizabeth after she learnt she was pregnant.

'My soul magnifies the Lord,
and my spirit rejoices in God my Saviour,
for he has regarded the low estate of his handmaiden.
For behold, henceforth all generations will call me blessed;
for he who is mighty has done great things for me,
and holy is his name.

And his mercy is on those who fear him
from generation to generation.
He has shown strength with his arm,
he has scattered the proud in the vanity of their hearts,
he has put down the mighty from their thrones,
and exalted those of low degree;
he has filled the hungry with good things
and the rich he has sent empty away.
He has helped his servant Israel,
in remembrance of his mercy,
as he spoke to our fathers,
to Abraham and his children for ever.'

Yours

Chõil

RORY BREMNER, *comedian*

Dear Michael

Not only does the Lord move in mysterious ways, but He's also on the Net.

As a result I've tracked down the hymn I was chasing which often runs through my head when things get tough.

I've also been searching for a reference for 'The Darkest Hour being before the Dawn', but it's only thrown up a bunch of websites of disturbing origin. But it's another image that comes to mind - usually in a tent at night with lions around, when you really do want to believe daylight isn't so far away.

It's a metaphor of course. But isn't everything these days?

Best wishes as ever

Yours

Say not the struggle naught availeth,
The labour and the wounds are in vain,
The enemy faints not, nor faileth,
And as things have been they remain.

If hopes were dupes, fears may be liars;
It may be, in yon smoke conceal'd,
Your comrades chase e'en now the fliers,
And, but for you, possess the field.

For while the tired waves, vainly breaking,
Seem here no painful inch to gain
Far back, through creeks and inlets making,
Comes silent, flooding in, the main.

And not by eastern windows only,
When daylight comes, comes in the light;
In front the sun climbs slow, how slowly!
But westward, look, the land is bright!

Arthur Hugh Clough (1819-1861)

NOEL BOTHAM, *author and journalist*

Dear Father Michael,

In 1966 I wrote *A Fighting Chance*, the story of the incredible journey by John Ridgway and Chay Blyth, who rowed across the Atlantic in 92 days.

I was particularly drawn to Chay Blyth. Two quotations he gave me became, and still are, of great inspiration to me in my own life.

He told me: 'I hate death and have very little time for prophecies and ill omens. There are a million things I have not done yet that I am determined to have a go at before I die.'

And he introduced me to his favourite quotation from Percy Shelley, which became my own.

> 'To suffer woes which hope thinks infinite,
> To forgive wrongs darker than death or night,
> To defy power which seems omnipotent,
> Never to change, nor falter, nor repent.
> This is to be good, great and joyous, beautiful and free,
> This alone, life, joy, empire and victory.'

My very best regards

LORD CALLAGHAN, *former British Prime Minister*

Dear Father Seed,

Thank you for giving Lord Callaghan a renewed opportunity to make a contribution to the book you are collating. He would like to send you the following verse by William Blake from *The Age of Innocence* for inclusion.

'To see a World in a grain of sand,
And a Heaven in a wild flower,
Hold infinity in the palm of your hand,
And Eternity in an hour.'

Yours sincerely

Gina Page
Private Secretary to Lord Callaghan

GEORGE CAREY, *former Archbishop of Canterbury*

Dear Father Michael,

It is in the context of anxieties, lack of hope and such fears about the future, both personal and universal, that we turn to look again at what the Christian faith affirms. The calm and assured message of the Bible does not disregard the realities of which these fears are the expression. But in facing them and interpreting them, it assures us that whatever the future holds, *God is*, and is as Bishop David Jenkins used to say 'as he is in Jesus'. The Christian hope does not depend on an almanac which gives us a date when Christ will return in victory; but it insists that we may rely on it. He *will* return. There *will* be an establishing in totality of his kingdom of love, light and justice, the mode of which can only be glimpsed in picture language. For beyond the Four Last Things - death so familiar and so unyielding, judgement so feared and rebelled against, hell expressing all that is ultimately most negative and destructive, and heaven, that dream of high delight in the immediate presence of God to be enjoyed for ever - beyond even these is the *Last Thing* of all, on which all depends: the immortal and eternal God.

'There, in that other world, what waits for me?
What shall I find after that other birth?
Not stormy, tossing, foaming sea,
But a new earth.
No sun to mark the changing of the days,
No slow, soft falling of the alternate night,
No moon, no star, no light upon my ways,
Only the Light.
No gray cathedral, wide and wondrous fair,
That I may tread where all my fathers trod,
Nay, nay, my soul, no house of God is there,
But only God.'

Mary Coleridge

+ George Cantuar

HILLARY CLINTON, *US Senator*

Dear Father Michael:

I am pleased to contribute with a favourite passage of mine from Jesus' Sermon on the Mount. These words have encouraged me throughout my life.

"And seeing the multitudes, he went up into a mountain: and when he was set, his disciples came unto him:

And he opened his mouth, and taught them, saying,

'Blessed are the poor in spirit: for theirs is the kingdom of heaven.

'Blessed are they that mourn: for they shall be comforted.

'Blessed are they which do hunger and thirst after righteousness: for they shall be filled.

'Blessed are the merciful: for they shall obtain mercy.

'Blessed are the pure in heart: for they shall see God.

'Blessed are the peacemakers: for they shall be called the children of God.

'Blessed are they which are persecuted for righteousness' sake: for theirs is the kingdom of heaven.

'Blessed are ye, when men shall revile you, and persecute you, and shall say all manner of evil against you falsely, for my sake.

'Rejoice, and be exceeding glad: for great is your reward in heaven: for so persecuted they the prophets which were before you.'"

Matthew 5: 1-12

With fellowship and appreciation for your good works, I am

Sincerely yours,

Hillary Rodham Clinton

TERENCE CONRAN, *style guru*

Dear Michael Seed,

I have chosen a wonderful passage written by Elizabeth David on Italian fish markets. Her beautiful style of writing has always greatly fascinated me, and I often refer to her work as a source of inspiration. Read this passage through, and by the end of it I can almost guarantee you will have the most incredible image of Venice in your mind.

'Of all the spectacular food markets in Italy, the one near the Rialto in Venice must be the most remarkable. The light of a Venetian dawn in early summer - you must be there about four o'clock in the morning to see the market coming to life - is so limpid and so still that it makes every separate vegetable and fruit and fish luminous with a life of its own, with unnaturally heightened colours and clear stencilled outlines. Here the cabbages are cobalt blue, the beetroots deep rose, the lettuces clear pure green, sharp as glass. Bunches of gaudy gold marrow-flowers show off the elegance of pink and white marbled bean pods, primrose potatoes, green plums, green peas. The colours of the peaches, cherries and apricots, packed in boxes lined with sugar-bag blue paper matching the blue canvas trousers worn by the men unloading the gondolas, are reflected in the red-rose mullet and the orange *vongole* and *cannestrelle* which have been prised out of their shells and heaped into baskets. In other markets, on other shores, the unfamiliar fishes may be livid, mysterious, repellent, fascinating, and bright with splendid colour. Only in Venice do they look good enough to eat. In Venice even ordinary sole and ugly great skate are striped with delicate lilac lights, the sardines shine like newly-minted silver coins, pink Venetian *scampi* are fat and fresh, infinitely enticing in the early dawn. The gentle swaying of the laden gondolas, the movements of the market men as they unload, swinging the boxes and baskets ashore, the robust life and rattling noise contrasted with the fragile taffeta colours and the opal sky of Venice - the whole scene is out of some marvellous unheard-of ballet.'

Hope this gets the gastric juices moving!

Best wishes

[signature]

JILLY COOPER, *novelist*

Dearest Father Michael,

… What a lovely idea for an anthology. I enclose a
copy of one of my very favourite poems by George
Herbert, it is called 'The Flower' and it shows that
even after great loss and intense unhapiness the heart
recovers and its owner is able to pick up the pieces.

…

  Who would have thought my shrivelled heart
Could have recovered greenness? It was gone
  Quite under ground, as flowers depart
To feed their mother-root when they have blown;
   Where they together
   All the hard weather,
Dead to the world, keep house unknown.

These are thy wonders, Lord of Power,
Killing and quickening, bring down to hell
    And up to heaven in an hour;
Making a chiming of a passing-bell.
    We say amiss,
    This or that is:
Thy word is all, if we could spell.

…

    And now in age I bud again
After so many deaths I live and write;
    I once more smell the dew and the rain,
And relish versing: O my only light,
    It cannot be
    That I am he
On whom thy tempests fell all night.

Lots of love,

FREDERICK FORSYTH, *novelist*

Dear Father Seed,

I feel that when it comes to passages of either prose or poetry that have always caused me to slip into a contemplative mood, there has never been anything to match Grey's 'Elegy in a Country Churchyard'.

There is a simple beauty about the way Grey uses language, an evocation of the timelessness of the land and of the unknown people who loved it and worked on it and who lie beneath the stones in his local churchyard.

It is a passage I am never able to read without thinking upon the futility of fame and fortune and the inevitability of the coming eternity. Simply reading these lines always manages to put any foolish notions I may have about success and wealth firmly back into perspective.

Sincere regards

Frederick Forsyth

JAMES HERBERT, *novelist*

Dear Fr Michael,

…I submit one old Chinese proverb that's always seemed right for me:

> 'Rather light a candle
> than complain about the darkness.'

Hope you are well and good!

Yours sincerely

James Herbert

JOHN GOWANS, *former General of the Salvation Army*

Dear Father,

It won't surprise you to note that the text which has always brought me the most comfort is that which is found in 1 Corinthians 1, 27a (KJV):

'God hath chosen the foolish things of the world to confound the wise.'

It has always been a matter of amazement to me that the Almighty seems to be ready to rely on very imperfect people in the achieving of His purpose. It is enormously comforting to discover the word 'chosen' in the passage which suggests that God has expressly decided to use the limited, the damaged, and the maimed as instruments in His hand for miraculous and often very beautiful projects.

Most servants of the Lord are conscious of their imperfections and often wonder, as I certainly do, why he does not look around for better people, nobler people, more capable people than myself. But as Paul clearly reminds us, the power of God is more clearly revealed when it is demonstrated and expressed in inadequate instruments.

Thank you for allowing me to comment, and I hope the above is of use to you.

Most sincerely yours,

SIR EDWARD HEATH, *former British Prime Minister*

Dear Father Seed,

Thank you for your letter.
I am glad that you like the text. It is one of my favourites.

With best wishes

Yours sincerely

A worthy Merchant is the Heir of Adventure, whose hopes hang much upon the Winds.

Upon a Wooden horse he rides through the World and in a Merry gale makes a path through the seas.

He is a discoverer of countries and a finder-out of commodities, resolute in his attempts and royal in his Expenses.

He is the life of traffic and the Maintenance of trade, the Sailors' Master and the Soldiers' friend.

He is the Exercise of the Exchange, the honour of Credit, the observation of time, and the understanding of thrift.

His Study is Number, his care his accounts, his Comfort his conscience, and his Wealth his good name.

He fears not Scylla and sails close by Charybdis, and having beaten out a Storm rides at rest in a harbour.

By his sea gain he makes his land purchase, and by the
Knowledge of trade finds the Key of his treasure.

Out of his travels he makes his discourses, and from his
Eye-observations brings the Model of Architecture.

He plants the Earth with foreign fruits, and knows at home
what is good abroad.

He is Neat in apparel, modest in demeanour, dainty in diet, and
Civil in his Carriage.

In sum, he is the pillar of a city, the enricher of a Country, the
furnisher of a Court, and the Worthy Servant of a King.

Nicolas Breton (1545-1626)

RICHARD INGRAMS, *writer, broadcaster, Editor of* The Oldie, *and former Editor of* Private Eye

Dear Fr Michael,

Here is my comforting passage for your collection:

> Two Chinamen, behind them a third,
> Are carved in lapis lazuli,
> Over them flies a long-legged bird,
> A symbol of longevity;
> The third, doubtless a serving-man,
> Carries a musical instrument.
>
> Every discoloration of the stone,
> Every accidental crack or dent,
> Seems a water-course or an avalanche,
> Or lofty slope where it still snows,
> Though doubtless plum or cherry branch
> Sweetens the little half-way house
> Those Chinamen climb towards, and I
> Delight to imagine them seated there;
> There, on the mountain and the sky,
> On all the tragic scene they stare.
> One asks for mournful melodies;
> Accomplished fingers begin to play.
> Their eyes mid many wrinkles, their eyes,
> Their ancient, glittering eyes, are gay.

From 'Lapis Lazuli' by W. B. Yeats

Please say a prayer for me

Regards

SIR EDWARD JONES, *Gentleman Usher of the Black Rod*

Dear Michael,

Many years ago I first heard these words as grace before dinner. Since then they have been tucked into the blotter on my desk to bring a sense of assurance and comfort, and to put the trials and tribulations of the everyday world into proportion.

> 'May the road rise to meet you,
> May the wind be always at your back,
> May the sun shine warm on your face,
> The rain fall softly on your fields,
> And until we meet again,
> May God hold you in the palm of his hand.'

Yours ever,

Edward Jones

NEIL KINNOCK,
politician, European Commissioner

Dear Fr. Seed,

The following quote has always had a special meaning for me:

We must not in the course of Publick Life expect *immediate* Approbation and *immediate* grateful Acknowledgement of our Services. But let us persevere thro' Abuse and even Injury. The internal Satisfaction of a good Conscience is always present, and Time will do us Justice in the Minds of the People, even of those at present the most prejudic'd against us.

Benjamin Franklin, written in 1772

Regards

COUNTESS OF LONGFORD, *author*

Dear Michael,

I should be honoured and thrilled to be included - it sounds such a lovely book.

I have got the most encouragement from a book called: *True Humanism* by Jacques Maritain.

I first read it when I was having difficulty in entering the Church, (which I longed to do) on scientific and political grounds. I greatly sympathised with the Humanists and utterly rejected General Franco.

Maritain was not only a great scientist but also Jewish and an ardent Roman Catholic.

Even if I only understood one word or one sentence in ten, that *one* was worth everything else put together.

He, Maritain, argued that Humanism was invaluable - but it had to be *true humanism*, and that was found within Christianity.

All best wishes from us both,

Elizabeth

EARL OF LONGFORD, *author and politician*

My dear Michael,

I suppose that the three quotations which have meant most to me from the Gospels are these:

1. I was in prison and you came to me.
2. The Son of Man has come to seek and to save those who are lost.
3. (from the Cross) Father forgive them for they know not what they do.

JOHN LE CARRÉ, *novelist*

Dear Father Michael,

In tough times I consult my wedding ring. Inside it, my wife, Jane had the engraver inscribe a line of John Donne:

'No Winter shall abate the Spring's encrease' [sic].

All good wishes,

John le Carré

SIR JOHN MORTIMER, *novelist and barrister*

Dear Father Michael Seed,

Two quotations and assurances. Life shouldn't be taken too seriously…

> 'When one subtracts from life infancy (which is vegetation) - sleep, eating and swilling - buttoning and unbuttoning - how much remains of downright existence? The summer of a dormouse.'
>
> *Byron*, Journals

> 'They say the seeds of what we will do are in all of us, but it always seemed to me that in those who make jokes in life the seeds are covered with better soil and with a higher grade of manure.'
>
> *Ernest Hemingway*, A Moveable Feast

CARDINAL CORMAC MURPHY-O'CONNOR,
Archbishop of Westminster

Dear Michael,

I would like to give the following words for your anthology of assurance. These words are taken from the Mass and are said by the priest. They have always given me great assurance in my years as a priest.

'Lord Jesus Christ, you said to your apostles: I leave you peace, my peace I give you. Look not on our sins, but on the faith of your Church, and grant us the peace and unity of your kingdom where you live forever and ever. Amen.'

Yours devotedly in Christ,

+ Cormac Murphy-O'Connor

CHRISTOPHER PATTEN, *European Commissioner*

Dear Father Michael,

The passage which has regularly inspired me is the last paragraph of volume one of Karl Popper's *The Open Society and Its Enemies*. It reads as follows:

'If we are tempted to rely on others and so be happy, if we shrink from the task of carrying our cross, the cross of humaneness, of reason, of responsibility, if we lose courage and flinch from the strain, then we must try to fortify ourselves with a clear understanding of the simple decision before us. We can return to the beasts. But if we wish to remain human, then there is only one way into the open society. We must go on into the unknown, the uncertain and insecure, using what means we have have to plan as well as we can for both security and freedom.'

Best wishes.

Yours

SIR ANGUS OGILVY,
businessman and husband of HRH Princess Alexandra

Dear Father Michael,

You wrote and asked me what passage or text has most encouraged and given me strength in times of difficulty. So far as the Scriptures are concerned - for me personally, and I suspect for many others - the words of the 23rd Psalm have always been immensely comforting and reassuring.

I have also never forgotten the former Speaker of the House of Commons - who later became Lord Tonypandy - telling me that when they were young they were so poor that their mother could not afford to buy them shoes. Understandably they were sometimes envious of other children - who seemed to be better off than they were. That was until one day - when he met a boy whose foot had been amputated as the result of an accident.

'Never again,' said George 'did I allow myself to indulge in self pity.'

When one gets down and depressed for whatever reason - it is well worth remembering that without exception there is always somebody who is worse off than oneself.

With kind regards -

Yours sincerely

EARL OF PERTH, *Peer of the realm and philanthropist*

Dear Father Michael,

It is hard to find the text you ask for 'strength in times of difficulty'. Surely this calls for prayer - not I suspect what you seek!

What about 'If you don't succeed at first, try, try again.' I know this is a hackneyed phrase but for me it more or less meets your request but one must beware in case 'obstinacy' is the outcome!

Best regards

Sincerely

David (Perth)

PRINCE RAINIER OF MONACO, *Sovereign of Monaco*

Dear Father,

I am delighted to bring my personal contribution to your noble cause.

Please find hereunder the prayer which has most inspired and encouraged me whilst giving me strength in times of difficulty:

> 'O God, grant me the serenity to
> accept what I cannot change, the
> courage to change what I can, and
> the wisdom to know the difference.'

I wish you every success in your endeavours.

My prayers are with you,

TIM PIGOTT-SMITH, *actor*

Dear Father Michael,

As a young actor, I found the disciplines of the theatre - the often unrewarding roles, the repetition - very hard to come to terms with. Then I remembered, and was often inspired by, a passage from J. D. Salinger's book *Franny and Zooey*

Franny is an aspiring young actress. Her attitude to acting is in crisis. Zooey, her brother, talks to her on the phone and reminds her of Seymour, their elder, now dead, brother, who created a fictitious 'Fat Lady'. Seymour's Fat Lady was someone for whom you did things - like polish your shoes when you were going to appear on the radio - if you didn't polish your shoes, no-one would see, but you were somehow letting the Fat Lady down! She is described as follows:

> '...sitting on this porch all day, swatting flies, with her radio going full-blast from morning till night...with very - you know - very thick legs, very veiny...I figured the heat was terrible, and she probably had cancer and - I don't know what.'

Zooey goes on...

'I don't care where an actor acts. It can be in summer stock, it can be over a radio, it can be over television, it can be in a goddam Broadway theatre, complete with the most fashionable, most well-fed, most sun-burned-looking audience you can imagine. But I'll tell you a terrible secret - Are you listening to me? There isn't anyone out there who isn't Seymour's Fat Lady. *There isn't anyone anywhere that isn't Seymour's Fat Lady.* Don't you know that? Don't you know that goddam secret yet? And don't you know - listen to me, now - *don't you know who that Fat Lady really is?* … Ah, buddy. Ah buddy. It's Christ Himself. Christ Himself, buddy.'

I love J. D. Salinger, and I drew great reassurance from this passage, which I have cobbled together a bit - I hope he will forgive me - in mitigation, I think the Fat Lady would!

Yours, with every good wish

Tim Piggot Smith

OLGA POLIZZI, *businesswoman*

Dear Father Seed,

I write this in haste as I am leaving for a ten day holiday - I am very happy to give you a text.

Footprints

One night a man had a dream. He dreamed he was walking along the beach with the Lord. Across the sky flashed scenes from his life. For each scene, he noticed two sets of footprints in the sand: one belonging to him, and the other to the Lord.

When the last scene of his life flashed before him, he looked back at the footprints in the sand. He noticed that many times along the path of his life there was only one set of footprints. He also noticed that it happened at the very lowest and saddest times in his life.

This really bothered him and he questioned the Lord about it. 'Lord, you said that once I decided to follow you, you'd walk with me all the way. But I have noticed that during the most troublesome times in my life, there's only one set of footprints. I don't understand why when I needed you most you would leave me.'

The Lord replied, 'My precious, precious child, I love you and I would never leave you. During your time of trial and suffering, when you see only one set of footprints, it was then that I carried you.'

LORD RUNCIE, *former Archbishop of Canterbury*

My dear Michael,

I have set out before you the words of St Theresa which are fairly well known. If this is too familiar or I have sent it for something else like *Will I See You in Heaven?* please ask me again. However, I am rather cumbered about with Holy Week at the moment and if this will suffice, I am very happy you should do whatever you like with it. You have been so kind to me and I am afraid this is rather a poor return.

With best wishes

Let nothing disturb thee,
Nothing affright thee;
All things are passing;
God never changeth;
Patient endurance
Attaineth to all things;
Who God possesseth
In nothing is wanting
Alone God sufficeth.

St Theresa's Bookmark

PROFESSOR JONATHAN SACKS, *Chief Rabbi*

Dear Father Michael,

The following passage, from the *Book of Psalms*, has been a source of strength to me at many difficult times. I dedicate it to the memory of the late Cardinal Hume, a true man of faith, who often told me that the *Book of Psalms* was central to his own sprituality:

'O God, You have examined me and You know:
You know me in my sitting down and in my standing up;
You have understood my thoughts from afar;
You watch my road and my rest;
You are familiar with all my paths.
Before any word is on my tongue,
O God, You know it.
You surround me, You are in front and behind,
And Your hand touches me.
This understanding is marvellous and too much for me,
It is high and I cannot grasp it.

Where shall I go from your spirit?
And where shall I hide from Your face?
If I go up into the heavens You are there,
And if I lie down among the dead You are there,
If I take the wings of dawn and live in the furthest
regions of the sea,
Even there Your hand will guide me and Your right
hand will hold me'.

(Psalm 139: 1-10)

Wishing you every success in your work.

PAUL SCHOFIELD, *actor*

Dear Father Michael Seed,

Thank you so much for your letter, please accept my apologies for my late response. I have been away from home for a short while.

It is kind of you to ask me to contribute to *The Gift of Assurance* and happily enclose a quote from St Thomas More's writings, which was a source of strength to me when in New York for a year, playing Sir Thomas in the play *A Man For All Seasons*.

I cannot claim that I underwent hardship during that time, but confess that I longed to be at home with my family.

I hope the passage will serve your purpose.

Give me thy grace, good Lord, to set the
world at nought.
To set my mind fast upon thee.
And not to hang on the blast of men's mouths;
To be content to be solitary;
Not to long for worldly company;
Little and little to cast off the world
And rid my mind of the business thereof.
Not to long to hear of any worldly things.
Gladly to be thinking of God,
To lean unto the comfort of God.

Sir Thomas More,
written in the margin of his prayerbook

Yours sincerely

NED SHERRIN, *broadcaster and author*

Dear Father Michael Seed,

Thank you for your letter. I send you the passage from the *Book of Common Prayer* which always seems to sum up all the requests for assurance which I fail to make.

'Almighty God, the fountain of all wisdom, who knowest our necessities before we ask and our ignorance in asking: We beseech thee to have compassion upon our infirmities; and those things, which for our blindness we cannot ask, vouchsafe to give us for the worthiness of thy Son Jesus Christ our Lord. Amen.'

Not much can slip through that net.

Sincerely

Ned Sherrin

MURIEL SPARK, *novelist*

Dear Fr Seed,

In reply to your letter I send you the following text which I have always held as a spiritual and philosophical truth, vital to the course of my life:

Ecclesiastes (Revised Version) 9,11:

> I returned, and saw
> under the sun, that the
> race is not to the swift
> nor the battle to the strong,
> neither yet bread to the wise,
> nor riches to men of
> understanding, nor yet favours
> to men of skill; but time
> and chance happeneth to
> them all.

With kind regards

Yours sincerely

Muriel Spark

SIR CLIFF RICHARD, *singer*

Dear Michael,

I submit the following text:

> 'For I am convinced that
> neither death nor life
> neither angels nor demons
> neither the present nor the future
> nor any powers,
> neither height nor depth,
> nor anything else in all creation,
> will be able to separate us from the love of God
> that is in the Christ Jesus our Lord.'

Romans 8, 28-29

With best wishes

Yours ever

JOAN SUTHERLAND, *opera singer*

Dear Father Michael,

I have sung the following lines many times in perform-
ances of Handel's *Messiah* and they have given me a
great sense of comfort and assurance.

> 'Come unto him all ye that labour, that are heavy
> laden, and he will give you rest. Take his yoke
> upon you, and learn of him, for he is meek and
> lowly of heart, and ye shall find rest unto your
> souls.'
>
> *Matthew XI, 28-29*

With best wishes

BARONESS THATCHER, *former British Prime Minister*

Dear Father Seed,

Perhaps the most reassuring and inspiring message one could find is contained in the words of the 23rd Psalm. But as I am sure that many people will choose this, may I suggest a verse from 'The Island', a poem by Francis Brett Young.

> What are you carrying, Pilgrims, Pilgrims?
>   What did you carry beyond the sea?

> *We carried the Book, we carried the Sword,*
> *A steadfast heart in the fear of the Lord,*
> *And a living faith in His plighted word*
>   *That all men should be free.*

Yours sincerely

ARCHBISHOP DESMOND TUTU,
former Archbishop of Capetown and Nobel Peace Prize Winner

Dear Father,

I have myself been very deeply encouraged by certain passages in the Bible, which one could conflate into each other. I cannot get over the wonder of Paul's statement, 'Whilst we were yet sinners, Christ died for us.' Because God chose me in Christ to be His child, before the foundation of the world, and predestined me to be adopted as one of His children through Jesus Christ. And that 'If God be for us, who can be against us?' For nothing, absolutely nothing can separate us from the love of God in Jesus Christ.

Those are words that speak of how precious I am in the sight of God; loved with a love that will not let me go - with a love that is unchanging and is unchangeable. And that I can do nothing to make God love me more, as I can do nothing to make God love me less. That's wonderful!

God bless you.

Yours sincerely,

THE GIFT OF ASSURANCE

CHAD VARAH, *founder of the Samaritans*

Dear Father Michael,

'Eye hath not seen, nor ear heard, neither hath entered into the heart of man, the things which God hath prepared for them that love Him.'

I am not good, but I do love him.

You didn't ask for something to look at, but I'll give you something never failing: The Sculpture of the Burghers of Calais, by Rodin, in Victoria Tower Gardens. The six men of varying ages were ordered by us British besiegers to come out of Calais in their shifts, with halters round their necks, and bearing the keys of the city, to be hanged. They express every human emotion one would expect, and Rodin captures these brilliantly. Queen Philippa pleaded for them and the King reprieved them, but Rodin shows them to us before her intercession.

I go and look at it several times a year.

Yours in O.B.L.,

Chad Varah.

BARONESS WILLIAMS, *politician*

Dear Fr Seed,

I am not sure the poem I have chosen repre-
sents assurance, but it does seem to me to provide a
strong sense of the divinity of Jesus Christ to those who
might doubt it. It also seems to me to address the mod-
ern, sceptical mind much more aptly than to earlier
professions of faith.

I hope your anthology proves to be a comfort
and source of strength to those who read and buy it.

Yours ever,

Friday's Child, W. H. Auden
(in memory of Dietrich Bonhoeffer)

He told us we were free to choose
But children as we were, we thought -
'Paternal Love will only use
Force in the last resort

On those too bumptious to repent' -
Accustomed to religious dread,
It never crossed our minds he meant
Exactly what He said.

Perhaps He frowns, perhaps He grieves,
But it seems idle to discuss
If anger or compassion leaves
The bigger bangs to us.

What reverence is rightly paid
To a Divinity so odd
He lets the Adam whom He made
Perform the Acts of God?

It might be jolly if we felt
Awe at this Universal Man
(When kings were local, people knelt);
some try to, but who can?

The self-observed observing Mind
We meet when we observe at all
Is not alarming or unkind
But utterly banal.

Though instruments at Its command
Make wish and counterwish come true,
It clearly cannot understand
What It can clearly do.

Since the analogies are rot
Our senses based belief upon,
We have no means of learning what
Is really going on,

And must put up with having learned
All proofs or disproofs that we tender
Of His existence are returned
Unopened to the sender.

Now, did He really break the seal
And rise again? We dare not say
But conscious unbelievers feel
Quite sure of Judgement Day.

Meanwhile, a silence on the cross,
As dead as we shall ever be,
Speaks of some total gain or loss,
And you and I are free

To guess from the insulted face
Just what Appearances He saves
By suffering in a public place
A death reserved for slaves.

BARONESS WARNOCK, *philosopher*

Dear Father Seed,

Here is one of my very favourite poems:

I struck the board and cried, No more!
   I will abroad.
What? shall I ever sigh and pine?
   My lines and life are free; free as the road.
   Loose as the winds, as large as store,
   Shall I be still in suit?
   Have I no harvest but a thorn
   To let me blood, and not restore
   What I have lost with cordial fruit?

Sure there was wine
   Before my sighs did dry it; there was corn
   Before my tears did drown it.
Is the year only lost to me?
   Have I no bays to crown it?
No flowers, no garlands gay? all blasted?
   All wasted?
Not so, my heart; but there is fruit
   And thou hast hands.

Recover all thy sigh-blown age
On double pleasures; leave thy cold dispute
Of what is fit and not; forsake thy cage,
   Thy rope of sands,
Which petty thoughts have made, and made to thee
   Good cable, to enforce and draw
   And be thy law,
While thou didst wink and would not see.
   Away; take heed;
   I will abroad.
Call in thy death's head there; tie up thy fears.
   He that forbears
To suit and serve his need,
   Deserves his load.
But as I raved and grew more fierce and wild
   At every word, Methoughts I heard one calling,
   'Child' And I replied, 'My Lord'.

George Herbert

Yours sincerely

Mary Warnock

75

ANN WIDDECOMBE, *member of Parliament and novelist*

Dear Michael,

Below is the prayer that I turn to most often.

> O Lord God, when thou
> givest to thy servants to
> endeavour any great matter,
> grant us also to know that it
> is not the beginning, but the
> continuing of the same, until
> it be thoroughly finished,
> which yieldeth the true glory.

*Prayer based on words by
Sir Francis Drake*

Yours sincerely

JOHN WILKINS, *Editor of* The Tablet

Dear Father Michael,

My greatest temptation has been despair. I am better than I was. One turning point came while I was watching birds on the island of Sheppey in the Thames. All day the black devil of depression had sat on my shoulder. But as I saw the clouds of waders turning as one over the water, I thought suddenly, 'it is all worth it'.

That sense now never leaves me. Faith, hope and love lead us into Life. But for those - most of us - afflicted at least some of the time in this way, there is one Bible passage so extraordinary in its reassurance that when I first read it I could hardly believe it:

> For if our heart condemn us,
> God is greater than our heart.
>
> *(1 John 3, 20)*

Yours

PHILIP ZIEGLER, *author and publisher*

Dear Father Michael,

I would like to put forward the Prologue to Bertrand Russell's *Autobiography* (published by Allen and Unwin, 1967).

'Three passions, simple but overwhelmingly strong, have governed my life: the longing for love, the search for knowledge, and unbearable pity for the suffering of mankind. These passions, like great winds, have blown me hither and thither, in a wayward course, over a deep ocean of anguish, reaching to the very verge of despair.

I have sought love, first, because it brings ecstacy - ecstacy so great that I would often have sacrificed all the rest of life for a few hours of this joy. I have sought it, next, because it relieves loneliness - that terrible loneliness in which one shivering consciousness looks over the rim of the world into the cold unfathomable lifeless abyss. I have sought it, finally, because in the union of love I have seen, in a mystic miniature, the prefiguring vision of the heaven that saints and poets have imagined. This is what I sought, and though it might seem too good for human life, this is what - at last - I have found.

With equal passion I have sought knowledge. I have wished to understand the hearts of men. I have wished to know why the stars shine. And I have tried to apprehend the Pythagorean power by which number holds sway above the flux. A little of this, but not much, I have achieved.

Love and knowledge, so far as they were possible, led upward towards the heavens. But always pity brought me back to earth. Echoes of cries of pain reverberate in my heart. Children in famine, victims tortured by oppressors, helpless old people, a hated burden to their own sons, and the whole world of loneliness, poverty and pain make a mockery of what human life should be. I long to alleviate the evil, but I cannot, and I too suffer.

This has been my life. I have found it worth living, and would gladly live it again if the chance were offered me.'

Yours sincerely,

ANONYMOUS

It is like looking at the back of a tapestry: one can see that there is a design but cannot discern what it is. It is only when we have left the world that we shall be able to see the beauty of the other side, and then we shall understand.

Teilhard de Chardin